TIME, TALENTS, THINGS

Books in the Woman's Workshop Series

Woman's Workshop Series

TIME, TALENTS, THINGS

STUDIES ON CHRISTIAN STEWARDSHIP

LATAYNE C. SCOTT

Lamplighter Books
Grand Rapids, Michigan
Zondervan Publishing House

TIME, TALENTS, THINGS:
A WOMAN'S WORKSHOP ON CHRISTIAN STEWARDSHIP
Copyright © 1987 by Latayne C. Scott

Lamplighter Books is an imprint of the Zondervan Publishing House,
1415 Lake Drive, S.E., Grand Rapids, Michigan 49506.

Library of Congress Cataloging in Publication Data

Scott, Latayne Colvett, 1952–
  Time, talents, and things.

  1. Stewardship, Christian. 2. Women—Religious life. I. Title.
BV772.S354   1987   248'.6'076   87-8291
ISBN 0-310-38771-X

All Scripture quotations, unless otherwise noted, are taken from the *Holy Bible:
New International Version* (North American Edition). Copyright © 1973, 1978,
1984, by the International Bible Society. Used by permission of Zondervan Bible
Publishers.

Argenteuil by Claude Monet
Cover Photo by SUPERSTOCK INTERNATIONAL
Cover Design by *The Church Art Works*, Salem, Oregon

Edited by Linda Vanderzalm and John Sloan

Printed in the United States of America

91 92 93 94 / CH / 10 9 8 7 6 5

This book is for
my beloved Friend
who invested Himself in me.

May my changed life,
My fervent love,
Be a noble return.

CONTENTS

Things

HOW TO GET THE MOST
OUT OF THIS STUDY

1. Determine to start a love affair with God's Word. Make a date with it—a regular study time each day—and commit yourself to it. Each lesson will lead you through a series of daily Bible readings about stewardship, but don't restrict yourself to those readings alone.

2. Pour out your heart to God in prayer every day. Discuss your daily wants and needs with Him, and trust Him to help you understand His Word.

3. Each lesson is divided into two parts—questions for group discussion and questions for individual, daily study, entitled "Exploring God's Word Through the Week." You will share your responses to the group discussion questions when your group meets together. You will do the "Exploring" questions on your own. Record your questions, insights, and responses to the daily questions in a small notebook.

4. The first lesson in this study explores the general

theme of stewardship. Each of the three sections that follow the first chapter discusses one of the three aspects of stewardship–time, talents, and things—and illustrates stewardship principles through the lives of characters from both the Old and New Testaments.

5. When you meet with your study group, be considerate of doctrinal views that are different from your own. Who knows, you could be wrong!

6. Don't come to Bible study "cold." Respect the group time enough to study the lesson before you come.

7. Be on time. Chronic lateness is a special form of selfishness.

8. Use a Bible version that is both easy for you to understand and technically correct in its translation. I suggest the New International Version. It is the version whose phrasing I have used in these study questions.

9. Commit yourself to stay on the subject, no matter how tempted you are to share interesting things that don't relate directly to the passage under discussion.

10. Always begin class with prayer.

INTRODUCTION

We give thee but thine own,
Whate'er the gift may be:
All that we have is thine alone,
A trust, O Lord, from thee.
—William Walsham How

The words of this hymn express a profound idea: all that we have belongs to God. Our time, energy, money, family, abilities, home, jobs—everything belongs to Him. Yet He has chosen to entrust these gifts to us. Most of us readily agree with this idea. But what we don't readily understand is that when God gives us time, talents, and things, they *still belong to Him.* He doesn't give up His ownership.

That's the key to understanding stewardship. A steward is a person who manages or administers property or a household *for someone else.* The steward doesn't own the property or the household. He or she merely cares for it on behalf of the owner or head of the household. The steward tries to manage the way the owner would manage; the steward cares for the household the way the master would care. The master gives the steward the tools, time, money, and resources to do the job effectively. The steward doesn't claim to own the tools or resources; they are merely in the steward's possession to use for the master's work.

So it is with us. God gives us time, talents, and things to use for His purposes, to do His work on earth. We are His stewards. He has entrusted to us all the gifts of the earth, and He expects us to manage His resources effectively.

We usually don't have trouble believing that God has given us these gifts, but we often have trouble using them wisely. Our difficulty comes when we fail to realize that stewardship means taking care of something that belongs to someone else and when we allow ourselves to be shaped by the world's view of time, talents, and things.

The biblical call to stewardship is radically different from the voices that tell us to grab what we can for ourselves, to hang on to what we have, to accumulate things for our own pleasure. Surely one of the hardest things about being a steward of time, talents, and things in the twentieth century is rearranging our thinking about our "rights." In this day of civil rights and violations, we have sometimes swallowed the world's lie that we have a "right" to do whatever pleases us and whatever doesn't offend a majority of people. We forget that to be a Christian is to be one who "has ceased to do what he likes and has dedicated his life to do as Christ likes," as William Barclay reminds us in his volume on Matthew. It is easy for us to hear the clamor of the world and forget the instructions of the Word. That's why studying the Bible's view of stewardship is so important.

Throughout the Bible runs a golden thread of stewardship, tracing a delightful pattern. From the beginning of time, God chose to appoint His children as stewards, caretakers of what

He owned. God appointed Adam and Eve as the first stewards when He gave them responsibility to care for the Garden of Eden. God also instructed Adam to name and take care of the animals, and later He gave him "hands on" experience with tilling the earth and helping it produce its abundance. This same gracious God, generations later, appointed Noah as His agent in protecting both animals and the human race from the destructive flood.

The thread continues as we see God appointing Abraham as a steward of the family that would grow to become His chosen people. Later we hear Moses teaching the Israelites how to be effective caretakers of the treasures God had given them. He reminds them that how they managed their lives demonstrated the proving of good versus evil, of life versus death. This theme continues throughout the time of the Old Covenant when the Jews were entrusted with the greatest possession of all: the Word of God. How they used it and abused it, treasured it and ignored it, cried for it and laughed at it tells us plainly what can happen to us if we do the same.

The thread leads into the New Testament where Jesus Himself exemplifies responsible stewardship. His first recorded words are those of a twelve-year-old boy sincerely and respectfully reminding His earthly parents that He had to be about His Father's "business." And how proud that Father must have been of the job His Son was doing, as the heavenly voice proclaimed, "This is my Son, whom I love; with Him I am well pleased."

The writer of the Book of Hebrews tells us that Jesus was tempted in all the areas that plague us, so we can expect that He, too, had to wrestle with how to handle time, talents, and things. When Satan tempted Jesus in the wilderness, he hoped Jesus would succumb to the desire for the material thing His body needed most—food—and turn stones into bread. Then the wily adversary tried to persuade Jesus to use

His talents or abilities to save Himself from falling from a great height. Finally Satan offered Jesus, to whom every knee will eventually bow, temporary ownership of the kingdoms of this world. The devil tried to get Jesus to bypass His time of suffering in which He would earn the right to be Lord of the earth. As we see Jesus fighting the same battles we daily wage over how to use what is within our grasp, we are strengthened by His strength, and comforted by the knowledge that just as angels came and ministered to Jesus after the temptation, so God will Himself supply all our needs as we fight off the adversary.

Stewardship is an overt theme in Jesus' teachings, especially in the parables He told. Jesus often illustrated a point by telling a story about a master or landlord or king who delegated money or authority to someone. He taught general principles in these ways, but sometimes He was very specific. In Luke 14:12–14, for example, He taught us that we are not good stewards if we give only to those from whom we expect a return.

Jesus' actions show us that He regarded time, talents, and things as gifts that should be used to benefit other people. In a short passage in Mark (2:23–3:5), our Savior recalled the story of David and his men eating showbread, and He illustrated that things are meant to be used for our real needs; He taught that talents are to be used for healing, not hurting; and He taught that the time is always right, even if it is a Sabbath, to help those who need it.

Throughout His life, by teaching and by example, Jesus showed His disciples that they were stewards of good gifts from a loving Father. He stressed the importance of being a servant, and illustrated this in taking the role of the lowliest household slave and washing the disciples' filth-encrusted feet. Then He revealed to them, and to us, the transformation that takes place when we humbly accept the role of servant:

"I no longer call you servants, because a servant does not know his master's business. Instead, I have called you friends, for everything that I have learned from my Father I have made known to you" (John 15:15).

It's wonderful to realize that these biblical characters were not the only effective stewards of God's gifts. We can see the principles of stewardship played out in the lives of Christians throughout history. It's also exciting to realize that each person's opportunities and resources for stewardship are different; each person is called to a unique stewardship. As Joseph F. Jones points out in his book, *Studies in Christian Stewardship*, "Men are not born equal, nor can they be expected to serve equally. But the service of the less gifted individual may be as pure and essential as that of the person with greater endowments."

But we are all equal in this: None of us knows when the Master will return. But we each have assigned tasks (Mark 13:33–34). Our great stewardship may be taking care of the people who depend on us: husbands, children, aged parents, friends, students. Paul certainly understood this, and his letters are full of instructions on how to treat husbands, wives, children, widows, and servants.

The New Testament uses two Greek words in the majority of its references to stewardship. The first, *epitrophos*, refers to a manager, foreman, or steward in a political sense—a governor or procurator. The more commonly used word, which interests me more, is the word *oikonomos*. The root of this word is derived from two Greek words: *oikos*, which means "home," and *nomos*, which means "law" or "management." In other words, stewardship at its very base means the management or administration of household affairs!

Now you can understand my excitement at presenting the concept of stewardship to women. We are stewards because we are entrusted with household affairs. Even those women who have careers outside the home still are stewards of their homes. This role of women in stewardship often has been ignored in seminars and teachings about stewardship. Lessons about stewardship frequently focus on the roles of men—both men in the Bible and men in the church today. And men do have important responsibilities to effectively manage what God has given them. But so do women.

Godly women have been effective stewards throughout history. Many biblical women not only realized that everything they "possessed" had come from God, but they also moved to the next logical step: they shared these assets with others. In fact, when I began researching this book, I wanted to call it "The Giving Place." That title occurred to me when I learned that the area of the temple where the contributions were made was the Court of the Women. The Bible is filled with examples of women who used their time, talents, and things in loving service to God and others: Rebekah at the well, heaving up heavy buckets of water for thirsty men and camels; Ruth gleaning fields in a foreign land for the mother of her dead husband; Abigail leading donkeys laden down with food into the desert to placate a king-to-be whom her brutish husband had insulted; the widow in Elijah's time who shared her oil and meal; the Shunammite woman who provided an apartment for Elisha; a trusting young virgin who endured a pregnancy that meant social disgrace and then raised a Child she never fully understood; Peter's mother-in-law, who waited on a houseful of men after she was healed; Dorcas, whose mourners showed Peter the fruits of her service-filled life even as they wept at her death.

All these women realized that God's ownership of their time, talents, and possessions meant that He trusted them when He *entrusted* them. Women—stewards of time, talents, and things. Just like you and me.

1

THE LORD OF TIME, TALENTS, AND THINGS

The steward does not give back to God "a portion" of what the steward owns, for God has never relinquished ownership.

—Joseph F. Jones

It is hard for twentieth-century Christians to remember that we are not owners but stewards of what God has given us. Although the world tells us that we are free to do what we please with what we have, the Bible tells us that all we have belongs to God and that we are to use His gifts for His purposes.

The studies in this book will help us understand what it means to be a steward and how we can more effectively use the time, talents, and things that God has given to us. As we have already discussed, a steward is a person who is appointed to manage or administer something for someone else. One of the steward's first jobs is to learn about the master or owner. Similarly, before we can understand our roles as stewards, we must understand who our Master is.

Read aloud Psalm 24:1.

  1. To whom does the earth belong? _____

_____

  2. If "everything" in the world belongs to God, what are some of the specific items in your life that belong to Him?

_____

_____

_____

Read aloud 1 Chronicles 29:10–14.

  3. a. According to these verses, what belongs to God?

_____

_____

_____

_____

  b. How does this truth conflict with our society's values?

_____

_____

_____

  4. What does it mean to you that all wealth and honor come from God? _____

_____

_____

5. What does David's comment, "Everything comes from you, and we have given you only what comes from your hand" say about possession? _____

_____

_____

Read aloud Romans 14:8.

6. What does it mean to you that you belong to the Lord?

_____

_____

Jesus knew we would forget that our Father, the Master, promises to provide all the resources we need for our task of stewardship. He knew we would lose perspective and begin to worry about things. In the following passage Jesus teaches His disciples about how (and how not) to spend their time and energy.

Read aloud Luke 12:22–34.

7. To whom was Jesus speaking? _____

_____

8. a. About what "things" did Jesus say the disciples were prone to worry? _____

_____

b. Are these "things" wrong? What was Jesus trying to point out to the disciples? _____

_____

_____

c. Do you think that in today's society we worry more about how we will get these things or about what the quality of these things will be? _____

_____

_____

_____

9. Whom did Jesus say would supply the necessities of life? If we work and earn the money to buy the things we need, how can we say that God supplies our needs? _____

_____

_____

10. What does it means to seek God's kingdom? _____

_____

_____

_____

11. How can selling our possessions free us from worrying about them? What did Jesus offer instead? _____

_____

_____

_____

12. What qualities of the Master are revealed in this passage? _____

_____

_____

EXPLORING GOD'S WORD THROUGH THE WEEK

Day 1. God is proud of us when we can "hold our own" with our time, talents, and possessions, right? Read Matthew 25:14–30.

Day 2. Read Proverbs 31:10−31 to see how one woman handled her time, talents, and possessions.

Day 3. Read Acts 8:9−25 to find out what happened to a man who tried to buy an ability with money.

Day 4. What does Colossians 3:17 have to do with the use of time? Talents? Possessions? Memorize this Scripture verse.

Day 5. Read Luke 10:30−37. Notice how the rescuer used his money. Did he show by this that he was concerned about the other man's past? His present? His future?

Day 6. It seems that it is difficult to set aside time for special projects, especially those that are to benefit others. For instance, we wonder if our homemade gifts are appreciated. How do you think the mourners in Acts 9:36−42 would respond to this kind of thinking?

2

WHAT THE MASTER EXPECTS

As if you could kill time without injuring eternity.

—Henry David Thoreau

An effective steward learns not only who the master is but also what the master expects. The steward's responsibility is to manage the business or household in the same way the master would manage it. The successful steward learns what qualities the master values and then works hard to exhibit those characteristics.

The exercises in this chapter explore the qualities that our Master expects of us: faithfulness, preparedness, diligence, productivity, willingness to work, and consistent work without procrastination.

Christ Himself was an effective steward of His time, energy, and work. He was very aware of the precious nature of the earth time allotted to Him to do the work of redeeming mankind. We can understand Jesus' resolute start to that ministry when we notice that He began it with a forty-day fast in which He communed with God and contemplated the work before Him.

Jesus had just twenty-four hours in each day, the same number we have. How did He use His time? If we look in Mark 1:35–39, we see how He began a day. He got up early in the morning, even before the sun was up, and went off alone to pray. He understood He had come to preach, and He understood that it would require planning and effort. He knew He had to go to the nearby towns to reach people; He couldn't do that by solitary prayer alone. Finally He followed through on His intentions and spent His time in preaching and healing. When He saw the great needs of the people who had followed Him, His time became their time.

Sometimes the work exhausted Him, and once He even fell asleep in a storm-pummeled boat. Perhaps it was experiences like this that caused Him to so tenderly rebuke the disciples who fell asleep as He agonized in Gethsemane.

Because He had to live under the tyranny of hours and minutes as we do, He can sympathize with our struggles. He plainly taught that it is never too late to begin to work for Him.

Read aloud Luke 12:35–48.

1. Who is the master mentioned in verses 35–40? What does it mean to be dressed for service and to have our lamps burning? _____

_____

_____

2. How will the master reward the faithful servants? What does that mean for us? _____

_____

_____

_____

3. Does knowing that Jesus will come at an unexpected time give you anxiety, or does it help you be a better steward? Explain. _____

_____

_____

_____

4. How would you answer Peter's question about the parable's audience (Luke 12:41)? _____

_____

_____

5. How were the servants in verses 42–45 dependent on the manager? How was the wise manager rewarded for his service? _____

_____

_____

_____

6. What does this parable say about a manager who in ignorance disobeys the master? _____

_____

_____

7. Explain why you think this is or is not a fair principle: "From everyone who has been given much, much will be demanded." _____

_____

_____

_____

8. Explain a situation when you gave your time and then it seemed that God expected you to give more. What relationship was there between the results of your giving and your attitude toward it? _____

_____

_____

_____

_____

9. What talents or abilities do you have? What do you think the statement, "From the one who has been entrusted with much, much more will be asked" says about talents?

_____

_____

_____

_____

10. If God will expect more of people who are blessed with material possessions, how can Jesus' teachings in Luke 12:22–34 help those of us who, by comparison with the rest of the world's population, are rich? _____

_____

_____

_____

Read aloud Matthew 20:1–5.

11. Jesus said that the kingdom of heaven is like the landowner hiring for his vineyard. If that is true, who would the landowner be? _____

_____

12. How much did the landowner agree to pay the first group of workers? How much did he agree to pay the workers hired at the third, sixth, and ninth hours? _____

_____

Read aloud Matthew 20:6–7.

13. What do the landowner's repeated trips to the market tell you about the amount of work to be done? _____

_____

14. What reason did the last group of workers give for why they hadn't worked all day? Explain why you think their excuse was or was not valid. _____

_____

_____

_____

Read aloud Matthew 20:8–16.

15. Why do you think the landowner asked his foreman to pay first the workers who were hired last? _____

_____

_____

_____

16. If you were one of the laborers who had worked all day, what would you have said to the master? _____

17. What two reasons did the landowner give for his decision to pay all the workers equally? _____

18. What do you think Jesus meant by His conclusion that the last would be first and the first last? _____

19. How would you apply this parable to the situation of two Christians, one of whom had been faithful all her life, and the other who had lived a worldly life but later had made a sincere decision to serve God? _____

20. In the situation above, what reasons would you give for not delaying in doing God's will? _____

EXPLORING GOD'S WORD THROUGH THE WEEK

Day 1. List some specific ways that Ephesians 5:15–6:9 says we can "make the most of every opportunity."

Day 2. What relationship does being "busy at home" have to the other desirable characteristics listed in Titus 2:3–5? What does Paul say is the purpose of such conduct (v. 5)?

Day 3. We've all heard the expression, "Time is money." Read the parable in Matthew 25:1–13 and imagine that the time each group of women had was indeed money. Would you say the issue here would be "unfair distribution of wealth" or "unwise investments"?

Day 4. Read 2 Peter 3:8–14. How is God's perspective of time different from ours? Why is He sometimes "slow"? What coming event should dictate our daily actions?

Day 5. Look at Titus 3:9, 14. What things does Paul regard as a waste of time? What does he suggest we can do to make our lives productive in God's sight?

Day 6. Read Proverbs 6:6–11. In your use of time this last week, were you an "ant"?

3

NEHEMIAH—OLD TESTAMENT STEWARD OF TIME

The most valuable thing a person can spend is his time.

—Theophrastus

The Jews' conception of time differed from ours in many ways. For instance, they perceived time in two segments: the "present age" of toil and trouble and the "coming age" of God's glory, which would take place after the "Day of the Lord" so often spoken of by the prophets. Their days did not begin at 12:01 A.M. as ours do; their days began at sunset and ended at the following sunset.

Amounts of time had great symbolic meaning to the Jews. Forty days, for instance, was a block of time that recurred throughout the Old Testament: the Flood, the embalming period of Joseph, Moses' stay on Sinai, Joshua's exploratory trip into Canaan, the length of Goliath's daily taunts of the Israelite army, Elijah's journey to Horeb, Nineveh's time of probation. In the New Testament, Jesus' fast in the wilderness and His stay on earth after His resurrection both lasted for forty days.

Forty years was also a significant time period: the time of wandering in the wilderness, Eli's judgeship of Israel, David's reign, and other blocks of time of peace and great adversity. The Jews celebrated each seventh year as a time of freedom, and each fiftieth year as a jubilee. These weren't just superstitious observances, they were reflections of the nature of their God. And as His work in the Creation shows us, even He was organized in His use of time.

If we look at Nehemiah, we see a man who was an effective steward of time—not because he was always busy but because he seemed to know the best ways to spend his time.

·Read aloud Nehemiah 1–2:10.

1. What does Nehemiah's reaction to the news he heard about Jerusalem tell you about him? _____

_____

_____

2. For what specifically did Nehemiah ask God (1:11)?

_____

3. From the month of Kislev to the month of Nisan was a period of four months. Why do you think Nehemiah waited so long to bring his request to the king? _____

_____

_____

_____

Read aloud Nehemiah 4.

4. Have you ever had a situation in which the best thing to do was to wait? Explain. _____

_____

_____

5. The wall was built in only fifty-two days (6:15). From chapter 4, we find some "managerial techniques" Nehemiah used to get this tremendous task done in such a short time. In the following chart, fill in the verse numbers that show where these techniques are described in this chapter.

Managerial Technique	*Verse # From Nehemiah 4*
Motivating others to work	
Dealing head-on with criticism and discouraging remarks	
Dividing tasks among workers	
Visibility and hard work of leaders	
Encouraging cooperation, not competition, among workers	
Encouragement to work long hours to see a task accomplished	
Leaders are a personal example of hard work	

Read aloud Nehemiah 8.

6. Do you think the people regarded spending many days listening to the Law being read aloud as a waste of time? Why or why not? _____

_____

_____

7. Why do you think the Levites had to explain the Law to the people? _____

_____

_____

_____

8. Read Ecclesiastes 3:1–8. What did Ezra, Nehemiah, and the Levites say that reminds us of this Ecclesiastes passage? _____

_____

_____

9. Are you satisfied with the amount of time that you spend in daily Bible study? If not, how can you change this situation? _____

_____

_____

10. For the next six days, keep a chart of how you spend your time. Put it on a 5 x 7 card or in a small notebook so you can keep it near you. At the end of the week, figure what percentage of time you spent in prayer, in Bible study, and in service to others (other than in regular household or vocational duties). Discuss with a Christian friend or prayer partner: 1) what changes, if any, you intend to make in your schedule and 2) how you can better handle interruptions and things that sidetrack you from good intentions. Ask the friend to pray with you about how to deal with these things.

EXPLORING GOD'S WORD THROUGH THE WEEK

Day 1. Read Genesis 29:1–28 to see how our attitude toward a certain task can make it seem to go faster.

Day 2. God instituted the Sabbath so people could rest. He also instituted "sabbath rest" times for the land they tilled. Read Leviticus 26:1–35 to see how this was to be accomplished with or without the cooperation of His people.

Days 3, 4, and 5. Read the Book of Esther (chapters 1–3, then 4–6, then 7–10). After each reading, note how Esther took advantage of time and used it to accomplish her goals.

Day 6. Has God ever changed His mind about the amount of time allotted to someone's life? Read 2 Kings 20:1–21. If you were granted a bonus of extra years on your life, how would you spend them?

4

PAUL—NEW TESTAMENT STEWARD OF TIME

Dost thou love life? Then do not squander time, for that is the stuff life is made of.

—Benjamin Franklin

William Barclay, in his Daily Study Bible volume on the book of Acts, shows us a side of a New Testament Christian worker that we might otherwise miss when we study the life of Paul. Barclay explains the passage in Acts 19:9–12, which tells of Paul teaching in the lecture hall of Tyrannus and of how handkerchiefs and aprons he had touched healed the sick. Barclay points out that one Greek New Testament manuscript said that Paul taught from 11 A.M. to 4 P.M. each day, which was "siesta" time in Ephesus. This meant that Paul had to work all morning and all evening at his trade of tentmaking in order to allow himself the luxury of teaching during those five hours. Furthermore, the handkerchief mentioned in Acts was actually the folded sweatband of a laborer and the apron that of a workman.

Let's see what Paul himself had to say about the way he used his time.

Read aloud 2 Thessalonians 3:6–10.

1. The Greek word for "idle" ("disorderly" KJV) is *ataktos* and refers to someone who is truant or "playing hooky." How does an idle Christian fit that description? _____

_____

_____

_____

2. Why do you think Paul used himself as an example of how the Thessalonians should spend their time? How do you think this made the Thessalonians feel? _____

_____

_____

_____

3. Read 1 Corinthians 9:1–15. Why do you think Paul argued so vigorously for an evangelist's right to be paid, and yet he said he had never used those rights himself? _____

_____

_____

_____

4. What advice do you think Paul would offer if he saw the welfare systems of the major countries of the world? _____

_____

_____

_____

Read aloud 2 Thessalonians 3:11–13.

5. How would you define "busybody"? What part does gossip usually play in the life of a busybody? _____

_____

_____

_____

6. Be prepared to take the role of either a busybody or a concerned Christian in the following situations:

a. What advice would you give to a friend who is a busybody? Act this situation out with another class member, then have class members who are not involved in the roleplay offer suggestions.

b. Does a Christian woman have the right to admonish another Christian woman who is a busybody but who is not a close friend? How would you handle this situation differently from the first situation? _____

_____

_____

7. Paul writes in verse 13 that we should not tire of doing what is right. Relate a situation in which you felt tired of doing right. _____

_____

_____

Read aloud 2 Thessalonians 3:14–15.

8. What was Paul's purpose, and what should ours be, in not offering fellowship to idle people? _____

_____

9. How does it affect you to be around a busybody? What techniques have you found useful in redirecting the conversation or actions of a busybody? _____

EXPLORING GOD'S WORD THROUGH THE WEEK

Day 1. Read Acts 20:2–3, 17–28. How long did Paul spend in Ephesus and how did he spend his time?

Day 2. Would an apostle waste time preaching to people who believed only in idols? Read Acts 17:16–33. How did this apostle use his listeners' belief in an unknown God to make the most of his opportunity to speak to them?

Day 3. Would the woman who had spent almost her entire adult life fasting and praying consider that she had wasted her time? (Look at Luke 2:21–38.)

Day 4. In Acts 1:1–8, what did Jesus tell the disciples about their responsibility to times and dates?

Day 5. If you were severely beaten and thrown into jail, what would be your priorities the first night you were imprisoned? What were the priorities of the men in Acts 16:16–34?

Day 6. Read Acts 20:7–12. What reasons could you give for why this young man fell asleep? Briefly review the amount of sleep you've had in the past week. Does the amount of sleep reflect good stewardship of your time? Of your body's energy? If not, what changes can you make this coming week?

5

TALENTS AND USEFULNESS

If my hand slacked, I should rob God.

— Antonio Stradivari

It is interesting that the word often translated as "hell" comes from Gehenna, the Valley of Hinnom. This valley, located just southwest of Jerusalem, had a long and loathsome history, for it was here that Ahaz taught the Israelites to worship the god Molech by sacrificing their own children as burnt offerings. Later, King Josiah decreed that this valley would be forever cursed, and it became a garbage dump for the city. For hundreds of years it smoldered with sooty fires that never seemed to go out.

Unlike our society, the society in ancient Jerusalem was not a throw-away culture. Clothes, household items, even scraps of papyrus were washed, repaired, patched, and used until they literally fell apart for the last time. Then, and only then, did the people throw something away, into Gehenna.

It's not surprising, then, that hell became connected in the Jewish mind with useless things.

The Bible teaches that no person is ever useless. Sometimes we think we are. We don't do things because we see ourselves as inept or unqualified. And no one can blame us for not doing a job that we are not qualified to do. But we can smell the rotting fumes of Gehenna when we know we should and can and could do a certain task—and we refuse to.

Part of our responsibility as stewards is to recognize what abilities God has given us and then be willing to use those abilities for His purposes.

Read aloud 1 Corinthians 12:1–3.

1. How would you define "talents"? _____

_____

_____

2. From reading these three verses, what general statement can you make about the source of statements regarding Christ's divinity? _____

_____

_____

Read aloud 1 Corinthians 12:4–11.

3. From what Paul said in verses 4–6, did he believe that being unified meant being uniform? Why or why not? What do all the gifts, services, and workings have in common?

_____

_____

_____

4. How do you know that these gifts are not just for our own personal benefit? _____

_____

_____

_____

5. List the gifts mentioned in verses 8–11. Check whether the gift was intended specifically for others or for oneself.

		Check one:	
Name of Gift	Verse #	For Self	For Others
1.			
2.			
3.			
4.			
5.			
6.			
7.			
8.			
9.			

6. Respond to this statement: "A Christian woman should decide what gift she thinks is best for her personality and then try to develop it." _____

_____

_____

Read aloud 1 Corinthians 12:12–26.

7. Describe a time when you felt like the foot in verse 15. How did you or can you resolve these feelings? _____

_____

_____

8. Give an example of a body part that seems to be weak but is actually indispensable. _____

_____

_____

9. Describe a Christian you know who fits the description of "weak but indispensable." _____

_____

_____

10. Give three reasons that show why a Christian could never say to other Christians, "I don't need you" (vv. 25–26). _____

_____

_____

_____

11. Many gifts are mentioned in verses 28–30. Does God make some special provisions for those who don't have any gifts? For people who have all the gifts? Why or why not?

_____

_____

12. Look ahead to chapter 13. What is the greater gift or more excellent way? Who can have this gift? List some specific ways that you can exercise this gift during the coming week. _____

_____

_____

EXPLORING GOD'S WORD THROUGH THE WEEK

Day 1. Was the apostles' ability to heal the sick a talent, an authorization, or both? Read Matthew 10:1; Mark 3:14–15, 6:7; and Luke 9:1. Does ability always follow God-given authorization?

Day 2. Read Romans 12:3–8. Does God measure the way we use our gifts qualitatively or quantitatively?

Day 3. Some people have "the gift of gab." What does James 3 say about the liabilities of this gift?

Day 4. God gave Solomon wisdom as a gift to help him govern his people (2 Chronicles 1). Read James 1:5–7 to see how we also can obtain it. If you need wisdom, follow the instructions.

Day 5. How does Matthew 5:13–16 apply to the use of our talents?

Day 6. How does 1 Peter 4:8–11 emphasize the relationship between our talents and the obligation to use them to serve?

6

MOSES—A RELUCTANT STEWARD OF GREAT TALENTS

If a man has a talent and cannot use it, he has failed. If he has a talent and uses only half of it, he has partly failed. If he has a talent and learns somehow to use the whole of it, he has gloriously succeeded and won a satisfaction and a triumph few men ever know.

—Thomas Wolfe

It's impossible to mention "stewardship" and "talents" in the same breath without thinking of the parable Jesus told in Matthew 25 of a master who gave three men currency called talents. Then, of course, the master called them to account for how they had managed that money in his absence. Because we use the same English word to refer to their monetary units and those special abilities we call talents, it's so easy to see the meanings seeping back and forth between the two.

Both in the story of these three stewards as well as in life, we know that if we don't use our talents, we lose them! And in today's Bible study we will see how even one of God's favorite people strained the Lord's patience by his reluctance to acknowledge and use his talents and resources.

Read aloud Exodus 3:1–10.

1. What was Moses doing when he saw the burning bush? Was this a profession for which he had had extensive training? _____

_____

_____

2. What indicates that God knew Moses? _____

_____

Read aloud Exodus 3:11–22.

3. What emotions do you think caused Moses to answer God the way he did (v. 11)? Describe a time in your own life when you were faced with a task or a situation that caused you to feel as Moses did. _____

_____

_____

4. How did God reassure Moses of success (v. 12)?

_____

_____

5. One way that God reassured Moses was by telling Moses in a very complete way who He was and what he intended to do in the lives of the Israelites (vv. 14–22). How can knowing God better and knowing His intentions for our lives make us better servants? _____

Read aloud Exodus 4:1–9.

6. Do you think that Moses was being stubborn in his question in verse 1, or do you think he was just logically anticipating obstacles? _____

_____

7. How did God answer Moses' question about the possible doubts of those to whom he would tell his story?

_____

8. How was Moses' staff like the talents that we each have?

_____

Read aloud Exodus 4:10–17.

9. How did God show that Moses' "ineloquence" was merely an excuse? _____

_____

10. Explain why you think that God's anger with Moses was justified or not justified. _____

_____

11. After reading about Moses, how do you think God feels about Christians who have abilities they won't use to serve Him or His people? _____

_____

_____

12. List some talents that you have or that other people have said you have. Note how you did or did not use those talents this week. Then write down a way that you can use at least one of those talents in the week to come.

Talent	Used Last Week?	How You Can Use It Next Week
1.		
2.		
3.		
4.		

EXPLORING GOD'S WORD THROUGH THE WEEK

Day 1. Read Deuteronomy 4 to discover what Moses said to the Israelites late in his life. Are these the words of a man who was not eloquent and who was "slow of speech and tongue"? What does this tell you about what happens when God tells us to do something we don't think we can do?

Day 2. Read Exodus 35:4–36:7. Where did these special talents come from?

Day 3. Does having a talent for leadership mean you must play an active role in all decisions that involve the people you are called to lead? Read Exodus 18:5–27.

Day 4. In Judges 6:1–16, what was Gideon doing when the angel came to him? What title did the angel give Gideon when he greeted him? What does this tell you about how God must see us?

Day 5. What events in Judges 7 caused Gideon to trust in God and not in his own "talents"?

Day 6. Spend time in prayer today asking the Lord to help you clearly see the talents He has given you. Ask Him to show you ways to use them in His service. Don't forget to praise Him for these talents.

7

PETER—A FRUITFUL STEWARD

A great bad man is worse than one of less talents, for he has the extended capability of doing harm.

—George Payne Rainsford James

One of the most misunderstood incidents in the life of Jesus occurred when He came upon a fig tree one day. When He found that it had no fruit on it, He caused it to wither and die. Our first reaction is to recoil distastefully from what seems to be an uncharacteristic display of destructiveness from the Lord of creation.

Herbert Lockyer's book *All the Miracles of the Bible* helps us understand this story. Apparently the Palestinian fig tree first produces a green fig in early spring and then later produces leaves. Mark says in chapter 11 that it was not the season for figs (Passover time was in April). For some reason this particular tree had budded out leaves early, but it had produced no fruit.

Its leafy branches were like a neon sign, saying "Look at me! I'm well along the way to harvest!" The leaves implied that it was bearing figs, since the fruit was supposed to precede the leaves. Thus, the tree was a visual lie.

The apostle Peter was with Jesus when this incident occurred, and surely it must have made a great impression on his mind. Throughout the Gospels we see the impetuous Peter revving up his spiritual engine and popping his reaction clutch without a firm grip on the steering wheel of his mind. He was the one who asked Jesus about the tree the next morning, and a few days later Peter declared, "Even if all fall away, I will not."

There was Peter, a barren fig tree waving his leaves, and a few days later when it was time to show fruit, he turned and ran.

You know, Jesus blasted that fig tree, and it died. But He didn't blast Peter—He forgave him and loved him and gave him chances to grow the fruit he wanted so sincerely to advertise. We begin to see a new Peter, transformed by the trust Jesus put in him, showing fruit by using the wonderful abilities God had given him.

Read aloud Acts 3:1–10.

1. Why, apparently, were Peter and John going to the temple? What does this tell you about them? ＿＿＿＿＿＿

＿＿＿＿＿＿＿＿＿＿＿＿＿＿＿＿＿＿＿＿＿＿＿＿＿

＿＿＿＿＿＿＿＿＿＿＿＿＿＿＿＿＿＿＿＿＿＿＿＿＿

2. How did Peter indicate by what he said to the lame man that his miraculous healing powers were something over which he was a steward? ＿＿＿＿＿＿＿＿＿＿

＿＿＿＿＿＿＿＿＿＿＿＿＿＿＿＿＿＿＿＿＿＿＿＿＿

＿＿＿＿＿＿＿＿＿＿＿＿＿＿＿＿＿＿＿＿＿＿＿＿＿

3. Have you ever been confined to bed or have you known someone who has been immobilized for an extended period of time? After that experience, could you or anyone else do what the man did in verse 8? What does that tell you about the nature of this healing? _____

_____

_____

4. How do you think the fact that this beggar was a well-known figure in Jerusalem affected Peter's decision to heal him? _____

_____

_____

Read aloud Acts 3:11–26.

5. How did the beggar make sure that the bystanders knew who had healed him? How did Peter identify the master of his stewardship of healing? _____

_____

_____

6. How did Peter use, to full advantage, the attention of the crowd who came running to him? _____

_____

_____

Read aloud Acts 4:1–12.

7. How did the message Peter preached bear fruit? _____

_____

_____

8. What did Peter tell the religious leaders about the "act of kindness shown to a cripple"? What kind of men did the religious leaders observe Peter and John to be? _____

_____

_____

9. Knowing Jesus made Peter and John resolute in their desire to serve Him; how can we as women "get to know" Jesus better? _____

_____

_____

10. Select a talent or ability you know you have and think of the last time you used it in a public or social situation. Fill out the following chart. Two examples have been done for you.

The Talent	Situation in Which the Talent Was Displayed	Who Got the "Glory"?	Result of Using the Talent
Peter/healing	Acts 3	"Not our power but God's."	rejoicing, conversions
Janice's secretarial skills	typing new church directory	"I organized it and did a neater job."	nice, new directory but feelings of former typists hurt; jealousy
(your talent)			

EXPLORING GOD'S WORD THROUGH THE WEEK

Day 1. Does having great talents or abilities prove that God approves of you or your use of those abilities? Read Matthew 7:21–23.

Day 2. Read Luke 10:38–42. What were the two talents that these women apparently had? Do you have either or both? Was either condemned? Was one said to be better? Why?

Day 3. Is it possible that God could require someone to lay aside hard-earned vocational experience and equipment to serve Him? Read what happened in Matthew 4:18–22. Do you think these men regretted their choice?

Day 4. Should we expect sometimes to feel drained when we are using our talents? Read Luke 8:40–56, noting especially verse 46. What do you think is a good way to replenish spiritual reserves when you feel that way?

Day 5. Your life will go smoothly if you are using your talents in the proper way, right? Read 2 Corinthians 11:22–28.

Day 6. Paul's scholarly training and heritage surely sharpened many of his intellectual talents. But what did he say was the most important knowledge he had? Read Philippians 3:3–14.

8

THE STEWARDSHIP OF THINGS

Earthly goods are given to be used, not to be collected. In the wilderness God gave Israel the manna every day, and they had no need to worry about food and drink. Indeed, if they kept any of the manna over until the next day, it went bad. In the same way, the disciple must receive his portion from God every day. If he stores it up as a permanent possession, he spoils not only the gift, but himself as well, for he sets his heart on his accumulated wealth, and makes it a barrier between himself and God. Where our treasure is, there is our trust, our security, our consolation, and our God. Hoarding is idolatry.

—Dietrich Bonhoeffer
The Cost of Discipleship

The phrase "God loves a cheerful giver" is the focal point of today's lesson, but it is tucked into a Scripture passage that is so rich in teaching about the stewardship of our material means that sometimes we just pass it over.

Whenever I think about a "cheerful giver," I recall the Greek word for "cheerful," *hilaron,* from which we get the English word "hilarious." I also think of my friend Helen Dayton.

While Helen was alive, she lived in a modest apartment that she continually redecorated. No, she wasn't a person who loved changing the decor of her home—quite the opposite. It was just that whenever she heard of someone who needed, say, a kitchen table or a couch or a coffee table, she just gave away hers. Then when the availability of her meager resources and a good garage sale happened to coincide, she would replace the item. How long it stayed in her house depended on when she heard of a need that it would fill. She was indeed a hilarious giver.

Helen was also an effective steward. She realized that her home and her furniture belonged to God. She merely managed them. If she discerned that someone needed a couch, she gave them the couch God had given her to care for. She realized that the couch wasn't hers but was God's. She was free to give things away because she never saw them as belonging to her in the first place.

Read aloud 2 Corinthians 8:1–9.

1. The word "grace" comes from a Greek word, *charisma,* which means "free gift." Read about the "free gift" in verses 1 and 2. Do you think the "free gift" referred to here was what the Macedonians wanted to give away, or does "free gift" refer to the *ability to give* that God had given the Macedonians? _____

_____

2. Based on verse 1, how would you advise a Christian who wanted to be able to give more to those in need?

_____

_____

3. Why were the Macedonians unlikely candidates for generous giving? _____

_____

_____

4. What "process" did the Macedonians go through in giving? _____

_____

_____

5. How was Jesus an example of the grace of giving?

_____

_____

Read aloud 2 Corinthians 8:10–15.

6. How can verse 12 help us when we feel that we are not giving as much as other people do? _____

_____

_____

7. What is the difference between what Paul talked about in verses 13–15 and the economic system known as communism? _____

_____

_____

Read aloud 2 Corinthians 9:6–11.

8. How would you answer someone who says, "What Paul said in verse 6 gives us a selfish reason for giving to others, since we are promised that we will be rewarded"? _____

_____

_____

9. What part does planning play in Christian giving? Does this rule out spontaneous giving? Why or why not? _____

_____

_____

10. How is the promise in verses 8–11 like a perpetual motion machine? _____

_____

_____

Read aloud 2 Corinthians 9:12–15.

11. What is the "bonus blessing" that Paul mentions in this section? _____

_____

12. If you can, share a time in your life that generous giving resulted in the blessings that Paul has outlined. Then, using the chart on the following page, list some similar needs that you could fill now.

EXPLORING GOD'S WORD THROUGH THE WEEK

Day 1. What additional reason did Paul give in Romans 15:26–27 for the Macedonians' generosity?

Day 2. What do 1 John 3:16–20 and James 2:14–17 say about the relationship of faith and love to giving?

Day 3. Read Luke 16:1–12. Do we gain friends for ourselves when we give away our money and material goods? To what degree does the friendship so gained depend upon our attitude in giving? What do you think are the "true riches" Jesus spoke of?

Day 4. How can we obtain the things we need in this life? Read Matthew 7:7–11.

Day 5. Look at 1 Timothy 6:3–5 to see the relationship between false doctrine and the idea that being a Christian is a way to become rich.

Day 6. What did Paul say in 1 Timothy 6:17–19 are true riches?

A Need	What I Can Do	Possible Obstacles	How to Overcome Obstacles
1.			
2.			
3.			

9

WHAT HANNAH KNEW

"I've decided," she said, *"that you haven't really given until you've given up something you desperately want to keep."*

—An anonymous woman
as quoted by Joe R. Barnett in
The People Who Tested God

I can honestly say that no Old Testament story affects me with more force than the story of Hannah. It is an inexhaustible mine of lessons. It is a story about jealousy, depression, desires, mistaken judgments, and vindication.

I can't read Hannah's prayer in 1 Samuel 1:10-11 without weeping for my own not-yet-fulfilled prayer requests. Although Hannah's story is a story about how God answers prayer, it is more a story about how we can respond *after* God has given us what we ask for.

We limit the power of this story if we see in it only a lesson about selfless motherhood. Hannah asked for Samuel with the specific intent of using him in God's service. What Hannah knew—even before she knew that she would have a son—was that she was accountable as a steward of that precious gift.

Read aloud 1 Samuel 1:1–8.

1. a. What indications do we have that this was a God-centered family? _____

_____

_____

b. What difficulties did the family have? Which, if any, of these difficulties have you experienced? _____

_____

_____

2. Whom does this passage say was responsible for Hannah's infertility? Who controls fertility today? _____

_____

_____

3. Elkanah's response, "Don't I mean more to you than ten sons?" perhaps indicates that he thought she should have been satisfied with just having him. Do you think Hannah should have been satisfied with her situation, or do you see her need for a child as separate from her need for a husband?

_____

_____

_____

Read aloud 1 Samuel 1:9–20.

4. How did Hannah show she believed that any child she might have would come from God? _____

_____

_____

5. Some people see Hannah's vow as a bargain with God. How can it be seen as a parent's stewardship of a child? ____

_____

_____

Read aloud 1 Samuel 1:21–28.

6. What do you know about Elkanah that helps you understand why he was willing to let Hannah take their son and present him to the Lord? _____

_____

_____

7. Make a list of your five closest friends (husband and children included, if they apply). Can you identify any specific times in the last month when you have treated them as your own "possessions" instead of freeing them to do things for God? What can you do to change these situations?

_____

_____

_____

_____

8. List some ways that you can "offer your children to God's service." (If you do not have children of your own, think about how you can prepare other children—nieces or nephews, neighbor children, children at your church, children of missionaries you know—to be used by God.)

_____

_____

9. If you are married, how have you and your husband resolved past conflicts about how to use things you have received from God? _____

_____

_____

Silently, as a group, read 1 Samuel 2:1–11.

10. Hannah's beautiful prayer focuses on one person. Who is it? Do you detect any feelings of self-pity after she gave up the son for whom she had prayed so fervently? _____

_____

_____

Read aloud 1 Samuel 2:18–21.

11. a. How did Hannah continue to take care of what she had given to God? _____

_____

b. Give an example of something you might give away but still in some way manage or care for. _____

_____

_____

12. a. How did God reward Hannah's actions with Samuel? _____

_____

b. Share an experience in which God rewarded your good stewardship of something He gave you. _____

_____

_____

13. List some things you ask God for on a regular basis. Select one thing from this list and commit it to the Lord's use and/or just to His glory in the coming week. Ask a friend to hold you accountable to your promise. _____

_____

_____

_____

EXPLORING GOD'S WORD THROUGH THE WEEK

Day 1. Read 2 Kings 4:1–7. What was the limit placed on the amount of oil the widow received? What relationship did this have to her faith?

Day 2. Read 2 Kings 4:8–17. What "assets" did this woman use to glorify God? What resources do you have to help a servant of God in your community?

Day 3. Read Judges 8:22–27 and 1 Samuel 15 to see how the improper stewardship of riches corrupted two great men.

Day 4. If you consecrate your wealth to the Lord, He'll be understanding of however you use it in the name of religion, right? Read Judges 17 and 18.

Day 5. What principles of stewardship did the Israelites have to put into practice as they gathered manna (Exod. 16)?

Day 6. Read Deuteronomy 8 and 1 Chronicles 29 to see what principles of stewardship Moses and David wanted God's people to understand.

10

NEW TESTAMENT STEWARDSHIP

If you find that you are becoming attached to some possession, consider giving it to someone who needs it. I still remember the Christmas I decided that rather than buying or even making an item for a particular individual, I would give him something that meant a lot to me. My motive was selfish: I wanted to know the liberation that comes from even this simple act of voluntary poverty. The gift was a ten-speed bike. As I drove to his home to deliver the gift, I remember singing with new meaning the worship chorus, "Freely, freely you have received; freely, freely give." Yesterday my six-year-old son heard of a classmate who needs a lunch pail and asked me if he could give him his own lunch pail. Hallelujah!

—Richard J. Foster

The new church that was formed on the day of Pentecost had in it Christians who expected Christ to return in the coming weeks or months. And, as we noted when we studied the passage in 2 Thessalonians 3, some people had even quit their jobs so they could devote themselves full-time to watching for Him!

We also noted that such people became a burden to the others—and surely the young church had enough problems just supplying the legitimate needs of the thousands who had given up homes, jobs, social position, and sometimes even pagan relatives to follow Jesus. How did they handle this perpetual crisis? Let's look at the Word and find out.

Read aloud Acts 2:42–47.

1. This passage describes the time just after the Day of Pentecost. What four things does verse 42 say were the focal point of the believers' lives? What are their twentieth-century equivalents?

Focal Points Then	20th-Century Equivalent	Am I "Devoted" to This? (Yes/No)
1.		
2.		
3.		
4.		

2. What relationship, if any, do you see between the fact that the believers were "together" and that they "had everything in common" (v. 44)? _____

_____

_____

3. What connection do you see between this passage and James 2:14–17? _____

_____

_____

4. What was the result of this "radical" behavior? _____

_____

_____

Read aloud Acts 4:32–35.

5. If we extend the imagery of verse 32 (they were of one heart and mind) and think of the church as a body (as we saw it in 1 Cor. 12), why was it logical that they would share everything? _____

_____

_____

6. How was the fact that "no one claimed that any of his possessions were his own" a reflection of stewardship?

_____

_____

7. How did the apostles assume a role of stewards?

_____

_____

Read aloud Acts 5:1–11.

8. What was the sin of Ananias and Sapphira? What might be a modern-day equivalent of this? _____

_____

_____

9. Do you think that God expects Christians today to sell their possessions to help others? Is there anything in your possession that you might need to sell or give away?

_____

_____

EXPLORING GOD'S WORD THROUGH THE WEEK

(Please note that following this section there is an appendix of additional questions for further thought and study. You are encouraged to pursue them because the Bible is rich in additional teachings on the subject of stewardship.)

Day 1. Saving for the future is always a good principle of stewardship, right? Read Luke 12:13–21. What was this man's purpose for saving up?

Day 2. How can you make sure that God won't "forget" about you? Read how one person's handling of his possessions kept him fresh in God's mind in Acts 10:1–8.

Day 3. Is it wrong to be very wealthy? Read Genesis 13:2 and Job 1:1–3. Is poverty always a virtue? Read Luke 15:11–20.

Day 4. Read Matthew 27:57–60; Luke 19:1–10; and John 19:38–40 for accounts of three very wealthy men who were disciples of Jesus.

Day 5. Do Christians have the right not to pay part or all of their taxes if they know the taxes will be spent on ungodly things? Read Matthew 22:15–22.

Day 6. Read Matthew 19:16–20. If you met someone who could truthfully claim to have kept the commandments as this man said he had, what kind of spiritual condition would you say that person was in? What was the person's dilemma? Do you think Christ intended His advice for all Christians?

APPENDIX—FOR FURTHER STUDY

1. Read Acts 6:1−7. How were these seven men stewards? How did their service allow the apostles to be better stewards of their time and talents?

2. Read Matthew 25:31−46. What elements of stewardship do you see in this parable?

3. Under what circumstances is the total destruction of a possession a good principle of stewardship? Read Acts 19:17−20.

4. What is the definition of "pure religion"? Read James 1:27. What does this have to do with stewardship?

5. Over what were the Jews given an exclusive stewardship as outlined by Paul in Romans 3:1−2? How are we similar stewards?

6. In Matthew 17:24−27, how did Peter get the money for the temple tax? What was Peter's profession? What principle of stewardship do you see here?

7. What principles of the stewardship of possessions did John the Baptist emphasize to the people who wanted to show that they had truly repented of their past sinful lives? Read Luke 3:7–14.

8. Why did Jesus tell the apostles not to take things along on their travels (Matt. 10)? What did this presuppose about the stewardship of the people with whom they would come into contact?

9. When Jesus condemned the Pharisees in Matthew 23, which of their offenses were related to irresponsible stewardship?

10. Read Genesis 12–15 and note how Abraham put principles of stewardship into practice.

11. Read Isaiah 58:6–14 and note some of the blessings promised to those who are good stewards of possessions.

12. What principle of stewardship did God emphasize to the Israelites when He told them in Leviticus 25:23 not to sell land "permanently"?

13. How were the women in Numbers 27 and 36 rewarded for their concern about their stewardship of their inheritance?

14. What principles of the stewardship of possessions are illustrated in Exodus 22 and 23?

15. How many literal stewards can you identify in the life of Joseph (Genesis 37–50)? How is Joseph a supreme example of the principles of stewardship?

God knew it would be difficult for us to be responsible stewards of His resources, especially when it comes to money. He knew that whether people had too much money or too little money, they would need help managing it well.

The following exercises reveal the Bible's perspective about riches, poverty, giving, greed, envy, etc. Exploring these passages will help us gain a more balanced perspective about how we are to handle the riches God has given to us.

1. What do we learn about riches and poverty from the letters to the churches in Smyrna (Rev. 2) and Laodicea (Rev. 3).

2. Read Acts 19:23–27 for the story of a man who gave some very "religious" reasons why his source of income should not be cut off.

3. We know that Joseph and Mary were not well-to-do because of the sacrifice they offered at the temple (see Luke 2:21–24 and Lev. 12:8). Now read Matthew 2. Where do you suppose they may have gotten the resources to make the trip to Egypt?

4. Is a weekly "collection" of money a custom or a commandment? Read 1 Corinthians 16:1–2.

5. Do ministers ("apostles" NIV) have a right to be paid? Read 1 Corinthians 9:1–14.

6. How was Paul able to have such a positive attitude even when he didn't have financial security (Phil. 4:10–13)?

7. We don't know much about the characters of the two men in Luke 16:19–31, but one was condemned and the other wasn't. Was the rich man condemned, do you think, for merely being rich?

8. What does Mark 4:19 say that the "deceitfulness of wealth" can do to the implanted Word in your heart?

9. How did Jesus say that giving to people who ask first as well as to those who just ruthlessly take from us makes us like God? Read Luke 6:27–36.

10. How are people who give to others without fanfare rewarded? Read Matthew 6:1–4.

11. What does Psalm 49 teach us about the value of riches?

12. What does Proverbs 23:4–5 say about riches?

13. When another Christian has defrauded you, it's best to have the issue settled by an impartial outsider like a judge, right? Read 1 Corinthians 6:1–8.

14. Does Matthew 6:24 say you can't have money and still serve God?

15. Is James 5:1–6 written about all rich people?

16. What does Hebrews 13:5–6 say about why we should not worry about lack of money?

17. Read Joshua 6–7 to see how one person's greed and disobedience caused the deaths of many people.

18. Read Genesis 26:12–33 to see how one servant of the Lord was able to handle problems with a business competitor. How is this similar to what Jesus said in Matthew 5:38–42?

19. Read 2 Kings 5 to see what happened when one man tried to be shrewd and ended up with a big problem.

20. When the Lord gave instructions on how wealthy a king might become in Deuteronomy 17:14–17, was He restricting or protecting kings (or both)?

21. How was the principle of "Corban" used by the Jews to justify greed (Mark 7:9–13)?

HELPS FOR LEADERS

1 / THE LORD OF TIME, TALENTS, AND THINGS

1. The earth and everything in it belong to God.

2. Help people see that their time, energy, health, personalities, families, jobs, car, homes, furniture, food, all belong to God—to be used for His purposes.

3. a. Greatness, power, glory, majesty, splendor, everything in heaven and earth, the kingdom, wealth, honor, strength, and power to exalt—everything is the Lord's.

b. Our society often tells us that we are the rulers of our own kingdoms. Honor and wealth are ours to earn and possess for ourselves. We are told that if we are successful at business, we are great.

4. Group members will have many ideas. Some may say that if all wealth and honor belong to God, then we don't need to be concerned about personal success, personal security, or prestigious jobs. Our questions are no longer,

"How can I have more (or less)?" but, "What does God want me to do with what He has given me?"

5. Believing this truth helps us to be openhanded with our time, talents, and things. We need not clutch possessively to what we have or greedily try to grab what we don't have.

6. Allow several people to share their personal testimony of what it means to belong to Christ, to be His possession.

7. Jesus was speaking to His disciples, drawing a conclusion from a story He had just told to a crowd. We, too, can consider ourselves to be His disciples in that we are trying to learn from Him and follow Him; what He said here can apply to us also.

8. a. Like us, the disciples apparently defined life in terms of food, drink, and clothing. And of course modern medical research bears out the truth of Jesus's statement that worrying will not add to our lives!

b. Jesus was saying that worry, not food and clothes, is what is wrong because worry implies a lack of trust in God.

c. The people of Jesus' time were often legitimately concerned with where their next meal would come from, whereas most of us don't have to worry about that sort of thing. More often we are concerned about how tasty or convenient a meal will be or how our clothes will impress others.

9. Jesus said that God will supply the things we need. Since He is the owner of all things, we should consider that the money we earn is our stewardship to do His will—and part of His will, of course, is that we provide for the daily needs of ourselves and our families as well as using our resources to help advance the work of the kingdom.

10. Class members will probably have many ideas about what this means, but one important element of seeking God's kingdom is making sure that we recognize who the King is— and obey His commands. Note, too, that seeking the kingdom and having possessions are not mutually exclusive. God promises that if we seek His kingdom, then He'll add what we need.

11. Some material possessions—especially those that require upkeep, repair, and monthly payments—are often in the long run more trouble than they are worth. I think Jesus was not asking the disciples to sell the necessities of life, but those things that would keep them from total service. Instead, Jesus offered the kingdom.

12. We learn that our Master is a loving, caring Father who values us highly. He knows all our needs and promises to supply them, even to the minutest detail. We also learn that He is eager to give us "His kingdom."

2 / WHAT THE MASTER EXPECTS

1. Verse 40 identifies the master as "the Son of man," a title that Jesus used to identify Himself. Being dressed and having lamps burning implies a conscious preparation for service, a planned willingness to use our abilities for whatever God needs done.

2. In this story the master rewards the faithful servants by waiting on them at a table. How humbling it is to realize that Jesus will invite us to His table and serve us, too, if we are faithful servants.

3. Since we don't know when Jesus will return, it encourages us to work at a consistent pace for Him. It also frees us from worrying about a deadline! Jesus also pointed out that anyone can be ready for something if that person knows that it will occur at a specified time. But faithful servants don't work in "spurts"; they work steadily. Of course, if we are not being faithful to our responsibilities, the thought of His return naturally will worry us.

4. Jesus answered Peter's question with a question, "Who is a faithful steward?" Peter's response would be that the disciples were certainly faithful. Christ's story encouraged them (and us) to keep on doing God's will, even when no one checks up on them.

5. The manager in this story was a steward in the fullest sense of the word—he was an *oikonomos* or household manager. He was in charge of the food allowances, and if he proved faithful, he would be put in charge of all the master's possessions. If, however, he was unfaithful and actually abused the people over whom he had authority as well as giving himself privileges he denied others, then he was punished. That was true in the case of the foolish manager who not only "lived it up" on his master's time but also beat the people under him.

6. Verses 47–48 make it plain that not doing the master's will is grounds for punishment. The servant who deliberately disobeyed the master was beaten "with many blows." The one who disobeys gets what he or she deserves—punishment—but less of it than the one who sinned deliberately. One important implication of this is that any servant should have the good sense to know basically what the master expects. This thought is borne out in Romans 1:18–20, where Paul makes the observation that no one can be excused by saying, "Well, I don't know what my master is like, therefore I don't know what he expects of me."

7. One thing that can help us understand this concept better is to remember that being entrusted with something means quite literally that someone trusts us to do the right thing with it. We can transfer this situation to our roles as parents: when we see our children carrying out responsibilities well, we usually give them more, not because we want to burden them down, but we want them to know the pride and confidence that come from accomplishing something. Conversely, if our children cannot or simply will not shoulder a responsibility, we owe it to them to punish them (so they won't learn the erroneous lesson that the way to have more free time is to evade our duties) and then we take away the responsibility, along with its compensations or rewards.

I had a boss in college who understood this very well. He often would ask me to do urgent, short-notice jobs, and when I would start to tell him that I was already busy, he would answer that that was why he had called me. He would say, "Busy people always find time to do things that need to be done, or they know how to delegate duties." And you know, he was right. I always got the job done, and part of the reason why is that I knew he trusted me to do it.

8. Be ready with a personal experience that will spark others' ideas. (Maybe my experience related in question 7 will be helpful.)

9. This question will help class members who don't know each other very well to become better acquainted. Emphasize that we are not boasting when we acknowledge that God has given us certain abilities.

10. Since we are, by the world's standard, very wealthy, we have the additional responsibility to share what we've been entrusted with. We must remember the promise that God will supply what we need, and He will supply all the more if we are helping others.

11. The landowner is representative of the Lord. Note how in this parable he is the master who delegates authority, money, messages, or possessions to others. This tells us something about God—He is no power-hungry honcho but someone who trusts His people.

12. The landowner promised to give the first group of workers a denarius. Then, verse 5 says he promised "whatever is right" to the second group of workers. We can assume he had the same agreement of "whatever is right" with the third and fourth groups (v. 5). The last workers were apparently hired without discussion of pay, perhaps implying that they were so happy to get the work that they didn't care.

13. There must have been a lot of work to be done. The master had to work, too—he made repeated trips to the marketplace to get workers. Perhaps this is because a) the first group of workers weren't getting the job done (either through poor work habits or because it was just too much for them); or more probably b) there weren't enough workers in the marketplace for the master to hire all at once. At any rate, the master was patient and kept going back again and again.

14. The last group of workers said they were in the marketplace because no one had hired them. Before we condemn them for laziness, we should remember that at least they were making themselves available for hire, being at the place where they could find employment instead of at home or at the local tavern.

15. This landowner was also a teacher. He wanted his workers to get to know him a little better—to see how he thought, and what "made him tick." From this story we can see that God is prepared to reward those who serve Him, either with specific blessings or with "what is right." He never compares us to others or shortchanges us, but considers us and our life situations on an individual basis. We also see Him as anxious to seek us out and give us an opportunity to serve.

16. Your response to this would depend on your concept of fairness—which was what the landowner had promised in the first place. He was trying to teach them about generosity, not about how to be what the world would call "business-like."

17. He had been true to his promise to pay a denarius.

Note that they didn't protest that they had been underpaid. According to Bible scholar William Barclay, a denarius was the normal, going rate for one day's labor. Their objection was apparently that the others had been overpaid. But the master replied that not only had he discharged his duty to the first groups, but also since it was his own money, he had a perfect right to distribute it as he pleased.

18. The last ones were so honored that they ended up being "first" in the eyes of the others. This made the others feel as if they had been put to "last place" behind them. In reality, though, were they not all paid equally?

19. It seems that this parable is teaching that the life-long Christian won't get any greater reward in heaven than those who are converted in old age. Of course, the life-long Christian won't have to live with the regrets of a life of sin, either. I'm sure that if you were to ask someone who had become a Christian late in life which way she would live life if she could do it over, she would say that she would not wait so long next time. I'm sure, too, that there will be a special measure of gratitude in that person's heart for the Lord who came one last time to the marketplace of her life and generously rewarded her as if she had worked all the time.

20. None of us has the assurance that we will ever see tomorrow morning's sunrise. Also, a life of sin has a terrible price—the toll on our bodies and minds sometimes is irrevocable. Shakespeare echoed this once when he said, "I wasted time, and now, behold! Time doth waste me."

3 / NEHEMIAH—OLD TESTAMENT STEWARD OF TIME

1. Point out that Nehemiah was a trusted court official of King Artaxerxes of Persia, who was the stepson of Queen

Esther. *Halley's Bible Handbook* suggests that Esther probably was still alive, which could account for why a Jewish man like Nehemiah could carry such political clout in the land of Persia. The Jews, who had been taken into captivity in 606 B.C., had returned to Jerusalem in 536 B.C. They had spent almost a hundred years trying to rebuild their temple and the wall of Jerusalem with no success. The story of Nehemiah begins in about 444 B.C.

Nehemiah's reaction to the news that his people were in disgrace and frustrated in their efforts to rebuild shows us not only that Nehemiah was a sensitive man but also that he deeply loved Jerusalem and its people. We also can see that Nehemiah was a man of action who dealt with problems directly. Note that he spent several days in mourning, fasting, and prayer. This was a pattern in his life—he always sought the Lord's will before embarking on any plan of action (see 4:4, 4:9, 6:9, 6:14).

2. He asked God to give him a favorable audience with the king.

3. Note that Nehemiah was the king's cupbearer—a fairly intimate position with a king, because a cupbearer had to be completely trustworthy to keep his master from being poisoned. The story in Genesis 40 of another cupbearer shows us that a cupbearer also was often a confidant and could even offer advice to a king.

King Artaxerxes knew Nehemiah well enough to notice a sad look on his face. The king trusted Nehemiah enough to grant him not only a leave of absence but also a letter of safe passage, free timber for building, army officers, and an entire cavalry! This was worth waiting for!

We must assume that Nehemiah knew his king well enough to wait for a favorable time to approach him. And, because of his practice of prayer and fasting, we can safely assume that he didn't spend those four months idly.

4. Be ready with an example from your own life or the life of someone you know.

5. He was a good motivator—"the people worked with all their hearts" (v. 6).

He dealt head-on with criticism and discouraging remarks (v. 14).

He divided up the tasks (v. 16).

Even high officials joined in the work and were visible to the other workers (vv. 16–17).

He encouraged cooperation, not unhealthy competition, among the different working groups (vv. 19–20).

He and the people worked long shifts to get the work done (v. 21).

He was himself a good example of hard work (v. 23).

6. We notice that the people listened "attentively" (v. 3). After years of captivity and then a hundred years of frustrating work, the people were grateful for the chance to hear the Law proclaimed. The wall was in fact built to give them protection so they could do this very thing—live and worship without fear. True, they could have spent their time "productively" building houses or working in the fields, but they knew their priorities: learning God's Word and praising and thanking God came first.

7. Perhaps during their years of captivity and harassment from their neighbors, they had not studied the Word and could not understand it.

8. This passage reminds us that there is a time for everything. The people had gone through a time of excitement and building, and though their hearts were now touched when they heard the Law, this special time was not to be spent grieving. They were to rejoice in the Lord their strength (v. 10).

9. Encourage the group not only to share their feelings about this important use of time but also to share thoughts about how each woman could organize her time to allow for these things. An inexpensive little book on this subject, *Manna In The Morning,* is available through any religious bookstore.

10. Make a mental note to ask at the beginning of the next class period the results of keeping the charts.

4 / PAUL—NEW TESTAMENT STEWARD OF TIME

NOTE: Spend a few minutes discussing the results of the charts that the women completed during the past week.

1. Many of the Thessalonians thought that Christ's return to this earth was so imminent that some apparently had quit their jobs and had settled down to wait for Him. To "play hooky" implies that you have responsibilities that you deliberately let "slide." Paul echoed this when he spoke of how such people weren't living according to the teaching he had given (v. 6).

So this was a willful idleness, not a lack of things to do. Just like children who play hooky, truant or idle Christians always end up with missed responsibilities catching up with them. Unfortunately, unlike schoolwork, life usually can't be made up.

2. Paul knew many of the Thessalonians personally, and his letters make us feel that we know him, too. We love Paul for his transparency, his willingness to open up his own past, "warts and all," for the instruction of others. He knew that he had faults, but he also knew that he had worked very hard at his trade of tentmaking as well as at his job as gospel preacher.

Paul wasn't trying to make the Thessalonians feel guilty.

He just wanted them to remember his hard work and to know that such work was actually beneficial to Paul—he felt good about not being a burden to those he loved.

3. Paul was a Rabbi (Acts 23:6, 26:5; Phil. 3:5) and as such was forbidden to take money for teaching; he had to be self-supporting. But in the new kingdom of which he was a member, the old laws didn't matter. Yet he would not take money he felt he didn't need if he was able to work at his profession. While he would deny himself that right, he wanted to make sure that people didn't refuse to help other ministers of the gospel who devoted their full-time efforts to the work of the kingdom.

4. Paul probably would say that anyone who wouldn't work shouldn't eat. But because of his special tenderness toward women, especially dependent widows, he would probably make provisions for them. It's hard to imagine Paul excusing an able-bodied man's refusal of a job he thought was "below" him in favor of a dole.

Be sensitive to the fact that women in the group may receive or may have received welfare payments. This may be because they are disabled, have been abandoned by their husbands, or have small children at home and have decided to raise them instead of getting a job that would not pay for both childcare and their living expenses. It is not our job to condemn anyone but to teach that Christian women should meet the needs of other Christian women wherever they can.

5. The dictionary defines busybody as "a person who meddles in the affairs of others." This kind of person is almost always a gossip, too. And gossip is a form of theft; it robs others of their time and reputations as the busybody pries into their lives.

6. Remind the group that the advice to the first person mentioned is to a friend, while the person in the second situation might be only an acquaintance. Ask for specific suggestions about how a person can deal with these situations without herself becoming a busybody.

7. Be prepared to tell how you have dealt with a specific situation (by getting rid of negative feelings, by getting others who need to be involved to share the load, etc.).

8. We want them to feel ashamed. Remember, feeling and accepting guilt for something we have done wrong is necessary before we can truly repent.

9. Encourage class members who perhaps have not had a chance to participate in the discussion to do so.

5 / TALENTS AND USEFULNESS

1. The dictionary defines talent as "a special gift, fitting one for a particular business, art, or profession." The word "gift" in this definition is especially appropriate because it ties it to the word "gift" that we see in 1 Corinthians 12:1, translated from the Greek word *charisma,* which means "an unmerited present from someone."

The gifts in 1 Corinthians 12:1 are specified as spiritual gifts, that is, abilities bestowed by the Holy Spirit. This lesson is not an appropriate situation to discuss whether or not the supernatural gifts such as tongues are present in the world today (not that this is not an important issue, just that it will put you so far off the track that you won't be able to make practical applications about our talents). The point should be made, however, that God gives us whatever abilities or talents that we have; we cannot take credit for them. It is, though, our responsibility to develop those gifts or talents to their fullest capacities and so honor God and serve others.

2. Paul was writing to the Corinthian Christians, many of whom had served idols in the past. He wanted them to know that acknowledging Jesus as Lord was essential.

The Greek word for Lord, *kurios,* was also the official title for Caesar. Jewish Christians were expelled from the synagogue and Roman Christians often faced death if they refused to curse the name of Jesus, the one Jews referred to as an apostate. When Corinthian Christians said that Jesus was Lord, they acknowledged Him as commander-in-chief of their whole lives.

Paul also wanted them to know that the ability to acknowledge Jesus as Lord was from God. This leads logically on to the next point in his discussion of the other kinds of abilities that God gives.

3. Paul is celebrating our differences, but he reminds us that all good gifts and abilities have a common source—God.

4. Paul emphasized in verse 7 that they are for the common good.

5. Paul's point is that all should be used for the common good. Probably the most obvious, though, is prophecy (v. 10). Prophecy in the New Testament doesn't mean foretelling the future as much as it means preaching, which, though it edifies the preacher somewhat, is most helpful to others (see 1 Corinthians 14:4).

6. Our PMA (Positive Mental Attitude) culture tells us we can do anything we set our mind to, but this passage teaches clearly that God chooses which gift to give us. The task of developing these gifts, however, rests squarely on our shoulders.

7. Be ready with an experience from your own life or the life of someone you know. Many such feelings were prevalent in most women during teenage years. Encourage shy members to respond, but don't press if they seem reluctant.

8. Some suggestions: the little toe, the eyelashes, the tiny bones in the ear. But each of these plays a role: balance, keeping dust out of the eyes, and hearing.

9. This might be a good time to mention the role of elderly Christian women who are unable to physically serve others but who are effective encouragers.

10. 1. God joined us all together as a unit. 2. The body should not be divided. 3. Our unity creates concern for one another because we are mutually dependent.

11. No one is without gifts. Even those who are severely retarded or even comatose (and if you're studying this book you don't fit into either category) help us by giving us an opportunity to serve in a selfless way.

12. Love—a gift we can all develop—has to be demonstrated in order to be perceived by others. Therefore, any ways of showing love that are mentioned by class members must necessarily involve some sort of action, not just "thinking loving thoughts" (even though those are important, too).

6 / MOSES—A RELUCTANT STEWARD OF GREAT TALENTS

1. Moses was tending his father-in-law's sheep. Moses had been brought up as a prince, and this was hardly the kind of work a prince was accustomed to. However, he had been in Midian for forty years (the same number that he had been a prince), so he was probably accustomed to his lifestyle. We have no scriptural indication that Moses resented this menial work or that he felt himself above it.

2. He called Moses by name. And, as following verses

showed, He knew him well enough to anticipate Moses' excuses and make provisions to overcome them.

3. Verse 6 tells us Moses was afraid of God. This, coupled with perhaps a poor self-image or even a reluctant fear of the future task, caused him to ask the equivalent of "Why me, Lord?"

Encourage class members to tell how they were able to overcome such feelings in the personal situations they relate.

4. God promised to be with Moses. In Romans 8:31, Paul carried this thought to its logical conclusion: "If God is for [with] us, who can be against us?"

5. God identified Himself as the God of Abraham, Isaac, and Jacob—in whose lives He had worked great miracles and whom He had repeatedly delivered from enemies. If we just can keep in mind the great power God has at His disposal, which He'll share with us if we do His will, we'll be less afraid to tackle "impossible" tasks that He wants us to do.

6. Allow differing opinions to be treated with equal consideration, since the Scripture does not say what Moses' motivation was. One thing is obvious, though—Moses was a tough nut to crack! Maybe that's the kind of person God needed for the monumental task ahead.

7. God is a God of action: He knew He had to convince Moses before Moses could convince anyone else.

8. Our talents, like Moses' staff, are something we have and which have great potential for showing the power of God. God asks us, "What is that in your hand?" of our abilities, too.

9. God pointed out that if He had the power to make Moses speak and hear and see, that He surely could help him speak and would tell him what to say.

10. After all those miracles and reassurances, we are a little annoyed with Moses too. But God is more gracious than most of us would have been: He gave Moses not only another chance but also a helper!

11. We are, as Romans 1:20 says, left "without excuse."

12. Encourage class members to make commitments to use their talents in specific ways.

7 / PETER—A FRUITFUL STEWARD

1. They were going to the temple to pray. They wanted not only to maintain contact with people but also to retain whatever Jewish customs did not conflict with their new knowledge of God's will. Also, many people were there—a great audience for God's Word, as following events would show.

2. A steward, you will remember, is someone entrusted with managing the possessions or authority of one above him or her. Peter had the ability to heal the man, but he understood the reason for his having that ability was to benefit others.

3. Since the man had been lame since birth (v. 2), he had never been able to walk and had to be carried wherever he went. The fact that his never-used legs and ankles could support him as he walked and leaped shows us how extravagant God's healing is.

4. Peter obviously focused in on this man for a reason. The fact that the man was well known would make him an undeniable witness of the power of God. Indeed, the bystanders "were filled with wonder and amazement" (v. 10).

5. After leaping and walking, the man clung to Peter and John. Peter showed that neither his own power nor his own righteousness had caused the healing; rather, God had healed this man in order to glorify His Son, Jesus.

6. He didn't use their attention to aggrandize himself but to turn glory to Jesus. He went on to show the people that they had a personal responsibility to repent of their part in the crucifixion of Jesus.

7. Verse 4 says "many believed."

8. Again Peter emphasized the purpose of the miracle: to glorify Jesus. The leaders saw that they were courageous, though "ordinary and unschooled." But the miracle itself, along with the men's unswerving testimony of experience with Jesus, was undoubtedly what stayed in the minds of the leaders.

9. The better we know Jesus, the more we want to be like Him. And if we are like Him, we are less likely to use our talents to aggrandize ourselves and more likely to use them to serve others and bring glory to God.

10. Encourage the class members to share what they have written in the chart. But remember that some people are not comfortable sharing personal experiences.

8 / THE STEWARDSHIP OF THINGS

1. Verses 1 and 2 say that the Macedonians were granted a *charisma* from God to be able to give generously.

2. If God granted this grace to the Macedonians, then we can feel free to ask God for the same *charisma* for ourselves.

3. They were very poor (v. 2). Even Paul said in verse 5 that their generosity was unexpected.

4. Verse 5 says that they took that all-important first step of giving themselves to the Lord. Then giving themselves to others must have been easier.

5. As verse 9 and Philippians 2:7−8 tell us, He became poor for our sakes but never stopped (or stops) giving to us.

6. Paul assured us that we shouldn't dwell on what we do not have but rather seek ways to be generous with what we do have.

7. Without passing judgment on nondemocratic political systems (after all, many Christians worldwide live under such systems, and Jesus and the New Testament Christians certainly did not live under a democracy!), point out one important difference: Paul advocated making economic conditions equal among believers through the voluntary contributions of individuals. In a modern communistic society, such equality is neither optional nor voluntary.

8. Paul is simply saying that blessings are a logical result of obeying just as a harvest is a logical result of sowing seed. Of course, if the reward becomes our motivation for giving, we are no better than the hypocrites in Matthew 6:1−2.

9. Paul said we should give what we have decided in our hearts ahead of time to give. Giving from the heart will eliminate any feelings of reluctance or compulsion. Spontaneous giving in addition to purposed giving is always a beautiful thing, and it is not at all ruled out by Paul's teaching on deliberate giving.

10. A perpetual motion machine is one which, once set into action, could keep itself going indefinitely. The cycle Paul describes—God gives us the ability to give; in response, we give to others; He rewards our generosity by providing us with more; we again are able to give to others—is like that kind of device. The problem most people have is in turning the "machine" on!

11. People will joyfully pray for someone who gives generously, and this, along with their increased love, is a bonus that can't be bought or coerced out of anyone!

12. The responses to this question will be a joyful

discussion experience, because Christians who have given generously will have a story to tell if they have searched their memories at all. Tap this enthusiasm to remind class members that filling the needs in others is always rewarding, in spite of obstacles.

9 / WHAT HANNAH KNEW

1. a. We have to be impressed with a man who would take his family to worship at the house of the Lord each year in an age when travel was difficult and inconvenient.

b. But like many Christian families today, Elkanah's family faced difficulties: infertility problems, family rivalries, depression, teasing, provoking, guilt, and feelings of inadequacy.

2. This passage clearly says that the Lord had closed up Hannah's womb. We should not understand this as a physical blockage of her uterus (although that could have been possible), but rather as a way of saying that the Lord had decided to delay her childbearing for His own reasons. Today, our technology allows us to prevent birth with birth-contol devices; we can also facilitate conception with devices unheard of a generation ago. We all know of babies born to mothers who conscientiously practiced birth control; many of us know a woman who is childless despite tests that prove she and her husband are physically capable of conceiving a child. In Hannah's day as well as today, it is God who ultimately decides when a life begins.

3. We can see that Elkanah may have fueled the fires of the rivalry between Penninah and Hannah by showing favoritism to Hannah, but we can also sense that he loved Hannah and wanted her to be happy. He needed the assurance that she loved him.

Human beings have a variety of needs, and no one person can completely satisfy all of these needs. In fact, it is a mistake to depend on a spouse or a friend to fill all our needs. I know one woman who has no friends other than her husband, and she clings to him parasitically. They are both miserable.

In Hannah's case, she felt she needed something she did not have. Her example of persistent prayer gives hope to those who may be healthy and well fed but who may be begging God for something else they feel they need. Hannah's example also may help us be more loving toward others when we pray for their needs that we may not understand.

4. In her desperation, Hannah went to God with her need, knowing that only He could fulfill the longing of her heart.

5. Some people may say that Hannah was bargaining with God (the Lord didn't seem to mind; He took her up on it), but I prefer to think that Hannah was telling God that she would be a good steward of any son He would give her. Her son would be used for God's glory. She didn't just promise to take him to church twice a week, but she promised to bring him up as a Nazarite—a person who would spend his whole life in service to God (see footnotes to v. 11).

6. We have already seen that Elkanah was a godly man who loved his wife and was concerned about her happiness. He undoubtedly understood her lifetime vow on behalf of their son, but we also know from Numbers 30:10–15 that he had the authority under the Mosaic Law to nullify that vow, if he chose to. Perhaps he gave in to Hannah's request because he had other sons (1 Sam. 1:4). But we shouldn't minimize that this was his son—and his beloved Hannah's only son.

Here is a beautiful and rare example of a joint decision

made by a husband and wife. This story is a great testimony to the power a godly woman can have in influencing her husband to use a blessing from God in a way that would glorify Him.

7–8. Be aware that personal experience and self-examinations are sometimes painful. Be ready with an example from your own life to "break the ice" on each of these questions.

9. You may want to ask an older Christian woman how she and her husband have handled this situation.

10. From start to finish the exuberant prayer focuses on God as the source of all her happiness. She never mentions her son directly, and mentions herself only in the context of being the recipient of God's blessings.

11. a. Hannah continued to stay in touch with her son, and she made clothing for him. She wanted him to know that she loved him and would not forget him, but surely her separating herself from him was a reminder that he was to be set apart for God's service for the rest of his life. We know this didn't damage him emotionally, for he grew up to be one of Israel's greatest prophets.

b. Even after parents release their adult children, they continue to care for them by serving them and perhaps advising them, but they must remember that they have released their children to do God's will. Those people who are not parents perhaps have other areas of their lives where they can be good stewards of things they have released from their care. Perhaps, like Hannah, we could ask the Lord for something—a pay increase, for example—and contribute that increase to a missionary fund or food bank. Then we could exercise our stewardship even farther by making sure that the money we gave was being used responsibly.

12. a. Verse 21 says the Lord was "gracious" to Hannah, abundantly blessing her with five additional children—and letting Samuel grow up in the very presence of God.

b. Be prepared to share an example of how God abundantly blesses us when we exercise responsible stewardship, make a sacrifice to Him, or fulfill a vow to Him.

13. Remind the group that stewardship of God's gifts doesn't always mean that we give that gift away. I use one of God's gifts to me—a word processor—to produce writings I hope will bless other women. I couldn't do that as effectively if I gave the computer away. Other women may cite examples of things that they use as "tools" in serving God.

10 / NEW TESTAMENT STEWARDSHIP

1. They spent their time in the apostles' teaching, fellowship, breaking of bread, and prayer. Today's equivalents would be reading and hearing the Word (as in Bible study and preaching), spending time with other Christians, communion and/or common meals, and prayer.

2. Hearts are more easily touched by the sufferings and poverty of another if we actually can see that person regularly. And if we're living with such a one, we would be hard-hearted indeed to ignore them if we are wealthy.

3. The James passage tells us what to do and why (we help other people because actions are a natural outcome of faith), and the Acts passage gives us a practical way to achieve this: by selling possessions to fill the needs of others.

4. The non-Christians around them looked on them with admiration because of their love for each other, and every day there were new conversions because people liked what they saw and wanted to be part of this wonderful phenomenon.

5. When we are reminded of our study of 1 Corinthians

12, we know that it would not do any good to feed and warm only certain parts of the body and allow the other parts to starve and be exposed to the elements.

6. Stewards recognize that they do not own the things over which they are given responsibility.

7. They were responsible for distributing the money from the sales of homes and land.

8. Let's see first what their sin was not.

They were not condemned for selling their land, for giving the money, or even for keeping part of the money for themselves. As Peter pointed out, the land was theirs to do with as they wished.

Their sin was in pretending to be more generous or sacrificial than they really were. Furthermore, it wasn't just a slip of the tongue, it was a deliberate, preplanned deception.

A modern-day equivalent might be boasting about giving or intentions to give that we never follow through with.

Or it might be lying about cash contributions to church when you are making out your income tax forms.

Or maybe it would be pretending to sacrificially give up something that we did not want anyway.

9. Be aware that this question will bring about a wide variety of responses. Through your attitudes and words, set a tone in the discussion that will encourage class members to be honest.

Here are some questions that might help in guiding this discussion:

a. Was the selling of personal goods in the first century compulsory or voluntary?

b. Does being a good steward mean that you keep nothing for yourself?

c. Is it possible that some people today might be moved to give up all their possessions to serve others, while others might fill the needs of a few people around them—and both kinds of people be approved by God?

d. To what extent do our family situations and other circumstances dictate how we manage our personal possessions?